Trouble
at the
Tudor Banquet

by Emma Murphy
with Trio Tagarela

ed. Ruth Kenward and Mark Dickman

Starshine Music

www.starshine.co.uk

Brown Cottage, Glynleigh Rd., Hankham, East Sussex, England. BN24 5BJ.
Tel/Fax: +44 (0)1323 764334 e-mail : enquiries@starshine.co.uk

ISBN 0 9535513 8 5

Cover illustration by Matty Tristram.

Contents

Please note: all activity sheets are copiable, but only for the <u>sole use of the purchaser and his / her school</u> for educational purposes.

Please note: that the script and score are **<u>not</u>** photocopiable. A photocopiable master of the script for pupils is available at low cost from Starshine Music, as are masters for instrumental parts.

Notes

In the text of the play, modern day language has been used for most purposes. This is to make the script easier to learn for junior age children, for whom this play was originally conceived.

This package is designed with maximum flexibility in mind. The show may be put on either without any musicians, simply using the CD recordings for musical items, or with a few musicians playing along with the CD, or with musicians taking all the parts.

Scores for musical items include parts for tuned percussion. These are not authentically Tudor, of course! However, we felt that it was important to have a score available for this kind of instrument, as many schools would wish to have maximum involvement of children and resources.

For reasons of simplicity, embellishments in the recorder playing on the CD do not always appear in the score. We felt that experienced players would be able to manage these without them appearing in the score, but that the majority of players would find embellishments an unwanted complication.

Website Resources available free of charge via our website: **www.starshine.co.uk**

There are additional activities available on our own site, as well as links to other sites, which we have selected carefully to be of interest to educators and their pupils. Costuming of the show, for instance, is something with which many directors would appreciate help. A few costume drawings are included towards the end of this book, but there are many historical costume specialists on the net, and we have featured the best of these on our Tudor links page. The links and resources area of our site is expandable, and all contributions are very welcome! E-mail us if you would like to offer an item or suggest a link.

Narrative only version

The narrative only version of the play is available from Starshine Music in the form of a photocopy master.

All enquiries to: Starshine Music Tel / Fax +44 (0) 1323 764334
or e-mail us: info@starshine.co.uk

Director's Notes

Cast in order of appearance:

The Household
Mother
Father
Anne (daughter)
Robert (son)
Dance Teacher
Cook
Martha (servant)
Tilly (servant)
Household musicians (non-speaking)

Tom's House
Tom (son)
Harry (father)

The Market
Market Trader 1
Market Trader 2
Other market traders, as many as are available
                       (non-speaking)
Passers-by   (non-speaking)
Street musicians   (non-speaking)

The Banquet
Master of Ceremonies
Court musicians   (non-speaking)
The Queen
Guards   (non-speaking)
Guests, servants, dancers (non-speaking)

Costumes
Robert and Anne (and Mother & Father) need daywear as well as banquet costumes. Tom needs a jester costume as well as his poor boy outfit. Everyone else can manage with one costume. Some line drawings appear at the end of the book **(p. 58)** to give you some ideas, but detailed costuming information is available via our website.

Props
Household: Mother needs money in small cloth purse to give to Cook. Cook also needs a money bag. Baskets for the Cook, Martha and Tilly, Anne and Robert.
Recorders and other instruments for any miming musicians if you have no actual players.
Market: Food items (unless you are miming): bread, fruit, meat, cider, ale, bottle of spirit. Bread for Tom. Market traders may have a stall, or a basket made from a wide shallow cardboard box hung from the trader's neck with string.
Tom's House: Recorders for Harry and Tom. Harry needs a case for his.
Banquet: A throne for Queen Elizabeth. Table(s) spread with food. Some plates could be covered with salvers to save finding food props. A large centrepiece of some kind, floral would be easiest to make. Plastic goblets if possible. Juggling balls for Tom.

Stage Set
Needs only to be minimal. Location can mostly be indicated by what's going on in the action. The only exception is the need to set up a table for the banquet. This can be done comically just before the banquet scene, by having the Master of Ceremonies order other servants about while setting up the scene, using ad lib dialogue.

Director's Overview

Scene 1

Track 1   **Instrumental - Galliard**

Anne and Robert are preparing for their first banquet. Anne is excited, but Robert doesn't want to go. Their parents are worried that Robert might not behave well.

Scene 2

Track 2   **Instrumental - Les Bouffons**

Anne and Robert's dancing lesson. Robert is bored and un-cooperative. They also practise their singing.

Track 3 / 14 (demo)   **Song - Greensleeves (a)**

Scene 3

Mother gives the servants their instructions for shopping at the market. Anne & Robert go with them.

Scene 4

Track 15   **Song - Street Cries 'Cherries So Ripe'**

The market place. After the first bits of shopping are done, Cook, Martha and Tilly leave the children to look after the baskets for a moment. Robert and Anne meet Tom, and go off to play with him. Cook is furious to find them missing. They go off in search of the children.

Track 16   **Song - Street Cries 'Chairs To Mend'**

The children are found. They apologise, then try to make up, singing a song that Tom has taught them.

Track 4 (rec.) */ 17* (demo)   **Song - Make New Friends (a)** ...& repeat as a round with servants:

Track 18 (demo)   **Song - Make New Friends (b)**   <u>or in unison</u>, with

Track 5 (backing)

Scene 5

Tom asks his father to take him to the banquet. His father says no, but Tom has other plans.

Scene 6

Anne and Robert are dressed in their banquet clothes. Father and Mother go through some points of etiquette with them, eg. how to curtsey and bow. They have a last dance practice.

Track 6   **Instrumental - Susato's Pavane**

Scene 7

Master of Ceremonies orders servants to bring tables into place etc. to set the banquet scene.

Track 7 / 19 (demo)   **Song - Strike It Up Tabor**

The party begins. Queen Elizabeth makes a grand entry.

Track 8   **Instrumental - The Queen's Fanfare**

Track 9   **Instrumental - Galliard**

Anne and Robert spot Tom hiding behind a curtain. They know he shouldn't be there. They sing their song for the queen.

Track 10 / 20 (demo)   **Song - Greensleeves (b)**

The queen spots Tom who is in a jester's costume. Thinking he's her court jester, she commands him to entertain everyone, and of course he fails. She realises he is an imposter, and he is seized by her guards. Robert steps forward to defend his friend, and persuades the Queen to let Tom play his recorder for her.

Track 11   **Instrumental - Pastime With Good Company (a)**

The Queen pardons Tom, who is allowed to stay, and play with the court musicians.

Track 12   **Instrumental - The Queenes Alman**

Tom thanks Robert for coming to his assistance. Robert's parents are delighted that Robert has sorted out the trouble at the banquet instead of causing it, as they had feared he would do! Robert thinks Tudor Banquets aren't too bad after all!

Track 13 / 21 (demo)   **Song - Pastime With Good Company (b)**

Trouble at the Tudor Banquet

SCENE 1

Music – 'Galliard'   ⊙ Track 1

[ANNE and ROBERT are sitting on stage playing a game (perhaps Nine Men's Morris – see activity sheets). Enter MOTHER and FATHER.]

MOTHER	At last - the big day is here!
FATHER	Tonight you're going to your first banquet!

[ANNE jumps up. ROBERT slumps and looks sulky.]

ANNE	Oh Mama, Papa, I'm so excited! I'm going to wear my new dress at last! *(sighs soppily)* Ahhh..... it's so beautiful!
ROBERT	*(grouchy)* No it's not. You'll look <u>silly</u> in it. *(to audience)* GIRLS!
FATHER	Robert! Don't be so rude.
ANNE	*(to Robert)* No, I <u>won't</u> look silly!
ROBERT	Yes, you will…
ANNE	No, I won't…
ROBERT	Yes, you will…

[MOTHER interrupts them.]

MOTHER	Anne! Robert! Stop arguing. We have lots to do.
ROBERT	*(Whining)* Oh Mama, do I have to go? I don't want to wear my horrible outfit and I don't want to dance.
FATHER	Of course you must go. It's an honour for us to be invited to the Queen's banquet.
ROBERT	*(whining)* I know, but...
MOTHER	Enough, Robert! Go and get ready for your dancing lesson.

[Exit ANNE/ROBERT. MOTHER/FATHER shake heads as ROBERT goes.]

MOTHER	I do hope he'll behave himself tonight...
FATHER	I'm sure he will. Do you remember <u>our</u> first banquet?
MOTHER	Of course! That's where we first met, when we were only ten years old... ah!
FATHER	I was so nervous when I asked you to dance.

MOTHER	... and I got all the steps wrong, I was so excited!
FATHER	*(laughing)* Yes, I had sore feet after you trod on them all evening!

[MOTHER hits him playfully, then becomes serious again.]

MOTHER	I know Anne will sing and dance properly tonight, but I do worry about Robert...
FATHER	Don't worry, I'll have a word with him. Come on, we have lots to do today.

[Exit MOTHER and FATHER.]

SCENE 2

*[Music is heard as the lights come up. The HOUSE MUSICIANS are playing in the corner of the room. ANNE and ROBERT are watching their DANCE TEACHER explain how to do the dance steps. ROBERT is obviously bored. DANCE TEACHER speaks once the music stops. **Dance steps shown on p.47**.]*

Music – Les Bouffons   ⊙ Track 2

DANCE TEACHER	Now, children, can you remember what type of dance this is?

[ROBERT yawns loudly and noticeably.]

DANCE TEACHER	What was that Robert?
ROBERT	*(Bored)* Oh, what, sorry?
ANNE	*(Nudging him)* What dance is it, silly?
ROBERT	Oh... urrh...I dunno.
ANNE	I know, ma'am, it's the Pavane.

[ANNE looks smugly at ROBERT, as she knows she has the right answer.]

DANCE TEACHER	That's right Anne. Robert, I wish you'd pay more attention.
ROBERT	*(Mumbling)* Sorry ma'am.
DANCE TEACHER	Now Robert, can you clap the Pavane's rhythm? It'll help you stay in time.

[ROBERT, slouching , claps it almost inaudibly.]

DANCE TEACHER	Really Robert, I can hardly hear you. Stand up straight! Anne, clap it with him.

[ANNE/ROBERT clap the rhythm: long, short, short, long, short, short.]

DANCE TEACHER	Excellent! Now both of you, watch me one more time. *(Demonstrating)* You start with you left foot and the steps are: Left together, right together, left, right, left, right (going forward) Right together, left together, right, left, right, left (going backwards). Ready?

[ROBERT reluctantly shuffles over to ANNE, refusing to take her hand.]

DANCE TEACHER	*(Sarcastically)* We'll all just wait until Robert's holding his sister's hand, shall we…? *(then, once Robert takes Anne's hand, to Musicians:)* Thank you! We're ready!

Music – Les Bouffons ⊙ Track 2

[ANNE, ROBERT & DANCE TEACHER go through the Pavane steps, with ROBERT dragging his feet and trying to act as bored as possible, and ANNE concentrating hard and smiling.]

ANNE	I did it! This is such fun!
ROBERT	*(Under his breath)* Bor-ing…!
DANCE TEACHER	Sorry Robert, I didn't hear that…
ROBERT	Oh, nothing...
DANCE TEACHER	Hmm. Well, I think we should have a break now.
ANNE	Can we sing the song we are going to sing tonight? PLEASE!
DANCE TEACHER	That would be nice.
ROBERT	*(Under his breath)* Oh no!
DANCE TEACHER	Which one is it?
ANNE	Greensleeves – my favourite!

[FATHER suddenly enters.]

FATHER	Hello everyone! *(to Dance Teacher)* How are they getting on then?
DANCE TEACHER	Well, sir, Anne is dancing beautifully, but Robert could put more effort into it...
FATHER	*(Menacingly, walking over to him)* Oh, could he?
ANNE	*(interrupting)* We're about to sing 'Greensleeves', Papa.
FATHER	That would be nice. *(Menacingly)* But first I think Robert needs a little TEST.
ROBERT	*(groaning)* Oh Papa…
FATHER	*(pointing at him)* You, sir, are going to tell me who wrote 'Greensleeves'.
ROBERT	*(relieved)* Phew! That's easy! Queen Elizabeth's father, King Henry VIII.
FATHER	*(surprised)* Well done! All right, carry on with the singing, then!

[FATHER indicates to musicians, who begin to play. ANNE/ROBERT sing.]

Song - Greensleeves (a) ⊙ Tracks 3 / 14

ALAS, MY LOVE, YOU DO ME WRONG
TO CAST ME OFF DISCOURTEOUSLY.
AND I HAVE LOVED YOU SO LONG,
DELIGHTING IN YOUR COMPANY.

GREENSLEEVES WAS ALL MY JOY,
GREENSLEEVES WAS MY DELIGHT.
GREENSLEEVES WAS MY HEART OF GOLD,
AND WHO BUT MY LADY GREENSLEEVES.

FATHER	Well done. Now run along – mother wants you. She's talking to Cook.

[ALL exit.]

SCENE 3

[Enter MOTHER and COOK.]

MOTHER	His Lordship and I may be going to a banquet, but the shopping still has to be done!
COOK	Quite right ma'am. I said the same to Martha and Tilly.

[Cook turns as MARTHA & TILLY enter behind, carrying 2 baskets each.]

Oh they're good girls! Here they are with the baskets now!

MOTHER	Let's just go through the list one more time.

[MARTHA & TILLY put the baskets on the floor.]

COOK	We need ham and beef.
MARTHA	*(curtseying)* ...as well as ale and cider.
TILLY	*(curtseying)* We also have the fruit to buy, your Ladyship.
MARTHA	...and we have to get some bread.
MOTHER	Good! Now, here's some money.

[MOTHER gives COOK the moneybag.]

COOK	Thank you, ma'am.

[ANNE and ROBERT come running in.]

ANNE	Mama, PLEASE can we go to the market too?
ROBERT	*(Sarcastically)* Anything to get away from here.
MOTHER	*(with a firm look at Robert)* Only if you BOTH promise to be good.
ANNE	I promise. I promise.

9

MOTHER	Robert?
ROBERT	All right, I promise.
MOTHER	Very well, but you must stay close to Cook at all times.
ROBERT	*(bored tone)* Of course we will.
ANNE	Hooray! Let's go!

[ANNE skips out of the kitchen, ROBERT following. COOK, MARTHA & TILLY pick up baskets.]

COOK	We'll be on our way, your Ladyship. Come along Martha, Tilly…

[ALL exit.]

SCENE 4

[The marketplace. TRADERS sing out their street cries. Among the crowd is TOM, sitting in a corner cleaning his recorder, perhaps eating a crust of bread. **See page 48 for additional Street Cries***]*

Song – Street Cries ⦿ Track 15
'Cherries so Ripe'.

CHERRIES SO RIPE AND SO ROUND,
THE BEST IN THE MARKET FOUND.
THEY'RE ONLY A PENNY A POUND,
SO WHO WILL BUY?
CHERRIES SO RIPE AND SO ROUND,
THE BEST IN THE MARKET FOUND.
THEY'RE ONLY A PENNY A POUND,
SO WHO WILL BUY?

Song – Street Cries ⦿ Track 16
'Chairs to Mend'

CHAIRS TO MEND, OLD CHAIRS TO MEND!
MACKEREL, FRESH MACKEREL!
ANY OLD RAGS? ANY OLD RAGS?

CHAIRS TO MEND, OLD CHAIRS TO MEND!
MACKEREL, FRESH MACKEREL!
ANY OLD RAGS? ANY OLD RAGS

[Enter COOK, MARTHA, TILLY, ANNE and ROBERT.]

COOK	Now then, Miss Anne, you go over there with Martha and Tilly, and Master Robert, you had better stay with me.

[MARTHA & TILLY go to TRADER 1. COOK & ROBERT go elsewhere.]

10

TRADER 1	*(to Tilly)* What can I get you miss?
TILLY	Could we have two loaves of bread and some fruit please?
TRADER 1	Right you are. Pass me your basket.

[TILLY hands over the basket to be filled.]

TRADER 1	Anything else?
TILLY	No, thank you.

[TRADER hands back the basket.]

TILLY	Ooh! That's heavy! You can help me carry some of this, Miss Anne.

[TILLY puts some things into a separate basket and gives it to ANNE.]

MARTHA	Could you tell us who we should get our meat from?
TRADER 1	*(pointing)* The gent over there with the cap on.
MARTHA	Right, thank you.

[MARTHA, TILLY & ANNE go to TRADER 2.]

TRADER 2	What can I get you three lovely ladies?
MARTHA	Could we have some ham and some beef please?
TRADER 2	Right-oh. *(Putting it into another basket)* You'll need something to wash this down with!
MARTHA	Actually, we do need some cider and ale if you've got it.
TRADER 2	Of course I do my lovelies. *(Putting it into baskets.)* And here's a special bottle of spirit for you, on the 'ouse!

[MARTHA giggles and nudges TILLY]

TILLY	Why thank you. That'll warm us up later on.

[MARTHA, TILLY & ANNE wander until COOK & ROBERT rejoin them.]

COOK	Children, can you be trusted to look after the baskets for a few moments?
ANNE & ROBERT	Yes, Cook.
COOK	Stay here, then. We need to have a quick look at something over there *(pointing)*.

[COOK, MARTHA & TILLY move away.]

TRADER 1	Fresh bread! Lovely fresh bread!
TRADER 2	Best beef you can buy! Best beef you can buy!

[Other traders may call out to advertise their wares ad lib.]

ROBERT	I hate shopping.
ANNE	Oh, I don't. I love it!
ROBERT	D'you see that boy over there? He looks about our age, doesn't he?
ANNE	I suppose so. He's a bit dirty, isn't he?
ROBERT	I'm bored. Shall we ask him to play with us?
ANNE	*(shocked)* No! We promised mama we'd stay with Cook.
ROBERT	Don't be such a goody-goody! He's only over there. We'll be able to see Cook all the time, and we can still keep an eye on the baskets.
ANNE	Well….
ROBERT	Oh suit yourself. I'm going to go over to him anyway.

> *[ROBERT goes to TOM. ANNE hesitates then follows him, but stands back a little, listening.]*

ROBERT	Hello. I'm Robert. What's you name?
TOM	Tom. *(indicating the baskets)* Is there a party tonight then?
ROBERT	That's just our normal shopping! Though as it happens we are going to a stupid Banquet…
TOM	*(interested)* Is that the <u>Queen</u>'s Banquet?
ROBERT	Yes.
TOM	I wish I was going.
ROBERT	Why? It's going to be SO boring.
TOM	I'd love to play my recorder there, and eat lots of lovely food.
ROBERT	The food will be good, I suppose. And the Court Jester will be fun to watch. Apart from that it's just dancing and singing.
TOM	It sounds like fun to me. I'd love to watch the jester perform.
ROBERT	If you want to go so much, then why don't you?
TOM	I wish! I'd never be invited to something like that. *(With pride)* But my Dad's playing tonight - he's one of the Court Musicians. He plays in the Queen's Recorder Consort.
ROBERT	*(impressed)* Really? *(puzzled, looking at Tom's clothes)* Does he get paid much?

TOM	Not really, but he loves his job. I want to be a musician too when I'm older.
ROBERT	I bet he has to wear a silly outfit.
TOM	*(offended)* It's not silly, it's just smart.
ROBERT	Well I think banquet clothes are silly. All those uncomfortable ruffs and things.
TOM	You ought to be pleased with what you've got. I'd give anything to have the kind of life you have. We never have any money.
ROBERT	*(A bit embarrassed)* Yes, I suppose so. I've never really thought about it...
	[ANNE moves up to them.]
ANNE	*(To Tom)* I think you're quite right.
	[ROBERT pulls a face and turns his back on her.]
TOM	*(To Robert)* Who's she then?
ROBERT	That's Anne. She's my sister.
ANNE	Hello. It's about time someone told Robert to appreciate what he's got.
ROBERT	*(Gasping)* You are such a pain! *(To Tom)* She's such a pain! If you had to put up with her all the time...
	[ANNE folds her arms and shakes her head.]
TOM	*(Stopping Robert)* Er... Yes, I'm sure... I know – why don't we play a game?
ROBERT	Yeah, what?
TOM	How about 'Hide and Seek?
ANNE	Only if I get to hide!
	[ROBERT rolls his eyes.]
TOM	*(To Anne)* All right then, we'll give you to 10.
ROBERT / TOM	1,2,3...
	[ANNE runs off to hide. The children carry on with their game. Meanwhile, COOK, MARTHA & TILLY return.]
COOK	*(gasps)* Oh mercy! Where have those children got to? Can you see them?
	[They look around.]
MARTHA	No. Come on Tilly, let's go and look for them over there.
	[MARTHA & TILLY go off in search of ANNE & ROBERT.]

COOK	Oh, this is dreadful! We shall be hung, drawn and quartered if they're lost!

[The traders' exit is covered by repeated singing of the rounds as they go. This can either be a straightforward repeat of the first time through, or the songs can be put together as partner songs.]

Song(s) – Street Cries
'Chairs to Mend' and 'Cherries so Ripe'.

CHAIRS TO MEND, OLD CHAIRS TO MEND!
MACKEREL, FRESH MACKEREL!
ANY OLD RAGS? ANY OLD RAGS?

CHAIRS TO MEND, OLD CHAIRS TO MEND!
MACKEREL, FRESH MACKEREL!
ANY OLD RAGS? ANY OLD RAGS?

CHERRIES SO RIPE AND SO ROUND,
THE BEST IN THE MARKET FOUND.
THEY'RE ONLY A PENNY A POUND,
SO WHO WILL BUY?
CHERRIES SO RIPE AND SO ROUND,
THE BEST IN THE MARKET FOUND.
THEY'RE ONLY A PENNY A POUND.
SO WHO WILL BUY?

[Exit TRADERS & COOK. ANNE, ROBERT & TOM are left sitting on the floor, TOM playing on his recorder, or showing them how it works. MARTHA & TILLY approach them.]

MARTHA	There you are. We thought we'd lost you.
TILLY	Cook is furious!
ROBERT	But we were only playing a game.
ANNE	*(indicating Tom)* …with Tom. Tom's father is a musician, and he's playing at the Banquet tonight.
	[COOK storms up to them.]
COOK	You disobedient children! Where have you been?
ANNE	*(apologetic)* I'm so sorry, Cook. We're both sorry – aren't we Robert? *(Ingratiatingly)* Tom's taught us a new song. Do you want to listen to it?
ROBERT	It's called 'Make New Friends'.
ANNE	Because we've just made friends with Tom!
COOK	*(grudgingly)* Hmmph. Well at least you didn't get up to any mischief.

Song – Make New Friends (a) ⊙ Tracks 4 / 17

MAKE NEW FRIENDS, BUT KEEP THE OLD.
ONE IS SILVER AND THE OTHER GOLD.
MAKE NEW FRIENDS, FOR THEY ARE DEAR.
KEEP THE OLD ONES AND THE NEW ONES NEAR.

MARTHA	Well done! That was lovely.
COOK	*(teasing)* Unusual to see you enjoying a song, Master Robert!
ROBERT	*(embarrassed)* Yes, well…

COOK	…but we really must be going home now.
TILLY	Her Ladyship will be getting worried about you. Say goodbye to your friend.
ANNE	Bye, Tom, it was nice to meet you.
ROBERT	We'll look out for your dad tonight.
TOM	I'll tell him I met you. Goodbye.

[TOM leaves.   The others pick up their baskets and prepare to go home.]

ANNE	Robert, Tom said that song could be sung as a round. Shall we give it a go?
ROBERT	Nah, I can't be bothered.
ANNE	Oh come on Robert! I'll start, then you join in.

*[ANNE and ROBERT begin the round, then COOK, MARTHA & TILLY join in. They go off, singing. This is demonstrated in Track 18, but if you prefer the song may be performed in unison with **Track 5**]*

Song – Make New Friends (6) ⊙ Track 5 / 18

MAKE NEW FRIENDS, BUT KEEP THE OLD.
ONE IS SILVER AND THE OTHER GOLD.
MAKE NEW FRIENDS, FOR THEY ARE DEAR.
KEEP THE OLD ONES AND THE NEW ONES NEAR.

SCENE 5

[Enter HARRY, Tom's father, carrying his recorder and case.   He sits down and begins taking the recorder apart.   Enter TOM, still carrying his recorder.]

TOM	Hello Father! Are you getting ready for the banquet?
HARRY	Yes, I'm just packing away my recorder.
TOM	I met two children today who are going to the banquet tonight. They said they'd look out for you.
HARRY	That's nice.
TOM	Can't I come with you tonight?
HARRY	No son, I've already told you. You can't go without an invitation, and they're not going to invite the likes of us, are they?
TOM	But can't I play in the consort with you?
HARRY	No, son, you'll just have to wait until you're older.

TOM	*(disappointed)* Huh…
HARRY	If you practise as often as you can, you'll be good enough very soon.
TOM	I'm always practising my recorder. I'm sure I could play well enough already
HARRY	*(laughing)* You never give up, do you? Now, I'd best be going or I'll be late. *(hugging Tom)* Goodnight, Tom - see you in the morning.
TOM	*(despondently)* Goodbye Dad. Have a good time.
	[Exit HARRY. TOM folds arms & walks about, scuffing feet on the floor.]
TOM	*(Talking to himself)* It's not fair. Why should Anne and Robert have all the luck?
	[He carries on pacing around for a minute, then:]
TOM	*(suddenly)* I WILL go to the banquet! Nobody has to see me - I'll just creep in the back way and hide behind the curtains! Nobody'll know I'm there! *(pausing for thought)* All I want to do is listen to the music and see the party for myself. I won't be doing any harm… but how will I get in without being spotted?
	[He sits down, scratches head, making a show of thinking. Suddenly he has an idea, and jumps up.]
TOM	I've got it! I know just the way I'll do it! It can't fail! *(pauses, holding his recorder out and looking at it)* Should I take my recorder? It might come in handy. I'll take it just in case.
	[Exit TOM.]

SCENE 6

[MARTHA is tying TILLY's apron strings. Enter ANNE in her banquet dress.]

TILLY	Oh Miss Anne, you look beautiful in that dress!
MARTHA	Oh yes, you'll be the belle of the banquet!
	[ANNE twirls around in her dress, enjoying the attention. ROBERT enters.]
ANNE	It is beautiful, isn't it?
ROBERT	*(Muttering)* Not really.
TILLY	Oh master Robert, be nice to your sister.
MARTHA	He doesn't look so bad himself!
	[ROBERT scowls.]
ANNE	He'd look better if he smiled a little.
	[ROBERT pulls a face at her. Enter MOTHER and FATHER.]

MOTHER	Oh Anne, you look wonderful!
FATHER	*(Hugging her)* Just like a princess.
MOTHER	And doesn't Robert look handsome?

> *[ANNE giggles, ROBERT pulls a face.]*

FATHER	*(patting his shoulder)* Now, Robert, you may look handsome, but are you old enough to behave in public?
ROBERT	*(Muttering)* Of course, Papa.
FATHER	I hope so. You're not to let us down.
MOTHER	Let's check you can curtsey properly Anne. Keep your back straight, and your head up, and bend your knees.

> *[ANNE curtseys.]*

MOTHER	Beautiful Anne, just right.
FATHER	And Robert, when you bow, put your left foot forwards, bend your right knee and lower your head.

> *[ROBERT bows unenthusiastically.]*

FATHER	Keep your back straight Robert. Do <u>try</u> to look as if you're enjoying yourself.

> *[ROBERT does a better bow.]*

FATHER	That's better!
MOTHER	I think you should dance the Pavane for us now. You need to get used to dancing in your new outfits.
FATHER	Where is your dance teacher?

> *[DANCE TEACHER enters, followed by the house MUSICIANS.]*

DANCE TEACHER	Here I am, sir.
FATHER	Would you go through the Pavane with them one last time?
DANCE TEACHER	Very well, sir.
FATHER	I'll dance with Anne, and you dance with Robert, dear.
ROBERT	Oh no, do we have to?
MOTHER	Yes you do, now let's get started.
DANCE TEACHER	Right ma'am. Everyone get into their positions.

> *[They all shuffle into their positions.]*

DANCE TEACHER   *(turning to musicians)* Can we have an introduction, please?

Music - Susato's Pavane   ⊙ Track 6

[As they dance, Robert is still dragging his feet and showing he is bored.]

FATHER   *(to the musicians)* Very nicely played, gentlemen.   I'm sure the court musicians will do no better!   *(to his family)* And so – to the banquet!

SCENE 7

[MASTER OF CEREMONIES enters, shouting orders ad lib to servants, who bring tables/props into position, including a throne. Once all is in place, court MUSICIANS (including HARRY) enter and begin to play. GUESTS arrive and mill about, including ROBERT, ANNE, MOTHER & FATHER.]

Song - 'Strike it Up, Tabor'   ⊙ Tracks 7 / 19

STRIKE IT UP, TABOR, AND PIPE US A FAVOUR!
THOU SHALT BE WELL PAID FOR THY LABOUR!
(repeat)

TONIGHT WE'LL HAVE A BANQUET,
AND DANCE THE WHOLE NIGHT THROUGH.
WE'LL ALL SING OUT TODAY!
DANCING, SINGING, EATING, DRINKING,
WE'LL ALL ENJOY THE QUEEN'S BANQUET.
(repeat)

STRIKE IT UP, TABOR, AND PIPE US A FAVOUR!
THOU SHALT BE WELL PAID FOR THY LABOUR!
(repeat)

M. of CEREM.   My lords, ladies and gentlemen – Her Majesty Queen Elizabeth!

Music - 'The Queenes Fanfare'   ⊙ Track 8

[Everyone stands still as fanfare is played.   QUEEN ELIZABETH enters, nodding at people as she passes. They curtsey / bow slowly and reverently to her. After she sits on the throne, MUSICIANS stop playing.]

QUEEN   Welcome, everyone! Enjoy the dancing! Enjoy the royal musicians! Enjoy the feast!

Music - 'Galliard'   ⊙ Track 9

[The music is played quietly enough for speech to be heard over it. Everyone continues to mill about. SERVANTS serve up the food and drink.]

ANNE   This is so amazing! Can you believe the number of people there are here?

FATHER   *(looking at the audience)* Hundreds!

ROBERT	And look at all this <u>food</u>! I <u>will</u> enjoy that!
MOTHER	Now, don't eat too much. You don't want to be sick when you're dancing later on.
ANNE	The musicians are very good, aren't they Father?
FATHER	Yes they are.
ROBERT	I wonder if they'll get to eat any of this delicious food?
MOTHER	I doubt it, dear. *(to Father)* Shall we go and talk to the Duchess of Devon, my dear?
	[FATHER & MOTHER move away.]
ANNE	*(pointing at Harry)* Robert, do you think that's Tom's father over there? The one on the end.
ROBERT	Oh yes, he looks a bit like Tom, doesn't he?
ANNE	What a shame Tom couldn't be here too…
ROBERT	I know. At least then I'd have someone <u>interesting</u> to talk to.
	[ANNE ignores him.]
ANNE	This is all so wonderful!
ROBERT	I wonder when the Jester will appear and turn this into a real party?
	[ROBERT suddenly spots TOM hiding behind the curtains, nudges ANNE.]
ROBERT	Anne, look! *(pointing)* There's Tom! Over there! I'm sure of it!
ANNE	Where?
ROBERT	Look, behind the curtain!
ANNE	Oh yes!
	[They both make to smile/wave at him. TOM sees them and hides away.]
ROBERT	I know he saw us. But why did he hide like that?
ANNE	Because, silly, he's not supposed to be here. He must have sneaked in!
M. of CEREM.	Pray silence for Her Majesty the Queen!
	[ALL fall silent.]
QUEEN	My father, the late King Henry, did so love a banquet. I thought it would be fitting to hear his music sung and played tonight.
ROBERT	*(Under his breath)* Oh no!

QUEEN	Two special guests will sing for us. Where are Robert and Anne?
	[FATHER helps them up. ROBERT hangs back; FATHER shoves him.]
QUEEN	Ah – here they come, to sing King Henry's song 'Greensleeves'.

[ANNE walks shyly over to QUEEN ELIZABETH, while ROBERT is pushed forwards by FATHER. QUEEN ELIZABETH claps to the musicians to begin the introduction. Greensleeves (a) may be used if only one verse is needed, or, if using the full version (b), after the first verse the guests may dance, then join in on the final repeat. At the end, everyone claps.]

Song – 'Greensleeves' (b) ⊙ Tracks 10 / 20

ALAS, MY LOVE, YOU DO ME WRONG
TO CAST ME OFF DISCOURTEOUSLY.
AND I HAVE LOVED YOU SO LONG,
DELIGHTING IN YOUR COMPANY.

GREENSLEEVES WAS ALL MY JOY,
GREENSLEEVES WAS MY DELIGHT.
GREENSLEEVES WAS MY HEART OF GOLD,
AND WHO BUT MY LADY GREENSLEEVES.

QUEEN	Marvellous! How beautifully they sing! Wouldn't you agree?
	[All applaud / murmur politely. TOM looks from behind the curtain and raises a congratulatory thumb at them. We see he's wearing a jester's costume. QUEEN ELIZABETH also spots him and calls out.]
QUEEN	Ah! Now I see my Jester has arrived! Come out and amuse us, Fool!
	[Tom looks uncomfortable and reluctantly shuffles forward.]
ROBERT	*(stage whisper)* Oh no! *(nudging Anne)* Look!
ANNE	It's Tom! This means big trouble!
QUEEN	Jester, entertain us in true banquet fashion.
	[TOM has three juggling balls in his hands.]
ROBERT	He'll never do it!
ANNE	What can we do?
	[TOM tries to juggle but the balls drop onto the floor. ALL laugh, thinking this is part of the act. TOM plays along for a while, but can't juggle. The QUEEN's expression turns from amusement to fury.]
QUEEN	You're not my Jester: you're an impostor. Guards, seize him!
	[Everyone gasps. Two GUARDS grab TOM, taking his jester's hat off. Harry recognises him.]
QUEEN	Who are you?

[Silence. HARRY looks shocked, as do ANNE & ROBERT. ALL murmur.]

QUEEN Well, speak up for yourself, who are you?

TOM *(Stuttering)* M.. my n..name is T..Tom.

QUEEN And what do you think you are doing disguised as my jester?

[TOM is silent. ALL are uneasy. Suddenly ROBERT steps forward.]

ROBERT Please, Your Majesty, he's a friend of ours.
He just wanted to come to the banquet. He doesn't mean any harm!

ANNE *(moving beside Robert)* He wanted to hear us sing.
He must have crept in without anyone looking.

QUEEN And <u>stole</u> my jester's costume! He must go to the Tower!

[Gasps, then an uneasy silence. HARRY steps forward.]

HARRY Your Majesty, this boy is my son. Have mercy! He's only young…

QUEEN He entered the palace uninvited! He must be punished!

ROBERT Your Majesty, Tom is no jester, but he could play a tune for you on his recorder.
He's really very good. And he can play your father's song, 'Pastime with Good
Company'. Everyone knows it's your favourite.

QUEEN Hmmm… Very well. Entertain us, boy, and perhaps I won't punish you.

TOM Oh, thank you, your Majesty! I will do my very best.

[TOM joins the court musicians and plays the first part solo (or mimes).]

Music – 'Pastime With Good Company (a) ⊙ Tr 2 /11

QUEEN Very good boy! You have earned yourself a pardon.
Stay! Play with your father and the Court Musicians.

TOM *(delighted)* Oh, thank you, Your Majesty! *(Bows)*
QUEEN Now, to the party! Let us dance!

Music – 'The Queenes Alman' ⊙ Track 12

[Music is quiet enough to speak over. TOM crosses to ROBERT.]

TOM I'm so grateful that you spoke up for me.
She'd have sent me to the Tower, I'm sure!

ROBERT I know!

TOM And now, thanks to you, I'm playing in the consort! Thank you, Robert.

ROBERT	*(pleased)* Oh, it was nothing.
TOM	So, are you enjoying yourself?
ROBERT	Yes I am, actually! I'm surprised how much fun it is.
TOM	You see, I told you so. Don't always take what you've got for granted.
ANNE	Tom, you had us very worried just then, but I'm so glad you <u>did</u> sneak in!
TOM	Me too! Well, I'd better get back over there, or she really will kill me! Bye – and thanks again.
ROBERT	Bye, Tom.
ANNE	Bye, Tom.
FATHER	Robert. I must admit I expected some kind of trouble at this banquet, but I thought it would be <u>you</u> causing it!
MOTHER	And instead it was you helping to sort things out!
FATHER	Well done, Robert, we're proud of you.

> *[ROBERT smiles, bashfully.]*

ANNE	I think this is the best party I've ever been to!
ROBERT	Yes, it <u>has</u> been fun! Tudor Banquets aren't so bad after all!

Song – 'Pastime With Good Company' (b) ⊙ Tr 13 / 21

PASTIME WITH GOOD COMPANY
I LOVE AND SHALL UNTIL I DIE.
GRUCH SO LUST BUT NONE DENY,
SO GOD BE PLEASED SO LIVE WILL I.

FOR MY PASTANCE HUNT, SING AND DANCE;
MY HEART IS SET TO MY COMFORT
ALL GOODLY SPORT WHO SHALL ME LET?

[Everyone joins in, singing and dancing. All applaud at the end. 'Strike It Up Tabor' can be played again to allow the cast to take a curtain call.]

Tel / Fax: +44 (0)1323 764334   E–mail: info@starshine.co.uk
www.starshine.co.uk

 Notes On Musical Items

Galliard

Galliards were pieces where the dancers and musicians could show off their abilities, as they were lively dances in 6/4 time, characteristically beginning on the half bar with three crotchets. Keep a light feel.

Les Bouffons

Thought to be composed by Thoinot Arbeau (1519-1595). This is a stately dance, and the Pavane rhythm (minim, crotchet, crotchet) should be very clear and in time. Arbeau's 'Orchesography', published in 1589, remains the most detailed and valuable treatise on 16th Century dances as well as dance music. 'Les Bouffons' appears in this work, but it's not clear whether or not Arbeau wrote the piece himself.

Greensleeves

This courtly ballad is thought to have been written by King Henry VIII (1491–1547) possibly for Anne Boleyn – though this is uncertain. This is a sad song about unrequited love, but does not need to become a dirge! It should always be played very legato, whatever the tempo.

Street Cries

These are to be sung as if calling out to attract trade, so articulation of the words is very important.

Make New Friends

A seventeenth century round.

Susato's Pavane

A Pavane written by German music publisher and composer Tylman Susato (1500-1561). It appears in his book 'Danserye'. Crotchets should be kept light, and pulse should be very steady.

Strike It Up Tabor

Written by Thomas Weelkes (1575-1623), who was one of the greatest English Madrigalists of his day. 'Strike It Up Tabor' is one of his livelier madrigals, and should be played with a bright happy mood throughout. The first and last sections should have a lively feel, with light/short notes, while the middle section should be more legato.

The Queen's Fanfare

Written in 2002 by Emma Murphy. A grand trumpet fanfare effect is the aim, so it's important that the rhythm is neat and clear: accurate and nimble tonguing is required! On the CD recording, bars 5 , 6 & 8 have four semiquavers on beat two. The score has been simplified because of the technical difficulty in playing these, but the alternative is marked should you wish to attempt it!

Pastime With Good Company

Written by King Henry VIII, who as a young man loved to enjoy himself! The song is all about the pastimes which he enjoys, and which he won't be denied! 'Gruch so lust' translates into modern English as 'Grumble if you like' – Gruch is the origin of our word 'grouch'. Quaver upbeats should be played short to give the piece a lively feel.

The Queenes Alman ('Queenes' is the old spelling for 'Queen's')

Written by William Byrd (1543-1623). This piece appears in the Fitzwilliam Virginal book. A virginal is a small keyboard instrument a little bit like the harpsichord. Elizabeth I was a very good virginal player, and also played the lute. The Alman, or Allemand, was a court dance, and was usually one of the first to be danced during a banquet – hence its proud and stately character.

---

* When playing with the CD, your start point in the score is where the asterisk appears, i.e. after the introduction.

Galliard

Anon.
arr. Trio Tagarela

Track 1/9(Reprise)

With Spirit (♩.=65)

25

26

Les Bouffons

? Thoinot Arbeau (1519-1595)

arr. Trio Tagarela

Track 2

Stately (♩=170)

2nd Descant Recorder

Treble Recorder

Tenor Recorder
(*optional)

Triangle

D. Rec. 1

D. Rec. 2

Tr. Rec.

Ten. Rec.

Tri.

Tuned
Perc.

Greensleeves (a+b)

? Henry VIII (1491-1547)
arr. Trio Tagarela

Greensleeves (a): omit the repeat at bar 25
and cut straight to the 3rd. x bar.
Greensleeves (b): play as written, including all repeats.

Greensleeves (a)
⊙ Track 3/14

Greensleeves (b)
⊙ Track 10/20

Greensleeves (a): v.1 ROBERT+ANNE

Greensleeves (b): v.1 ROBERT   v.2 *Instrumental*   v.3 ALL

A - las, my love you do me wrong to

cast me off___ dis-cour-teous-ly; and I have lo - ved you so long,_ de - light-ing in___ your

com - pa - ny. Green - sleeves___was all my joy,_____ Green - sleeves was my de - light,

STREET CRIES

(a) – Cherries So Ripe

Anon.
arr. Trio Tagarela

Track 15

Moderato (♩=120)

Cher - ries so ripe and so round, the best in the mar - ket - found. They're on - ly a pen - ny a pound, so who will buy?

(b) – Chairs to Mend

Track 16

Moderato (♩=120)

Chairs to mend, old chairs to mend, mac - ke - rel, fresh mac - ke - rel, a - ny old rags, a - ny old rags?

© 2003 Starshine Music

31

(c) – Chairs to Mend/Cherries So Ripe

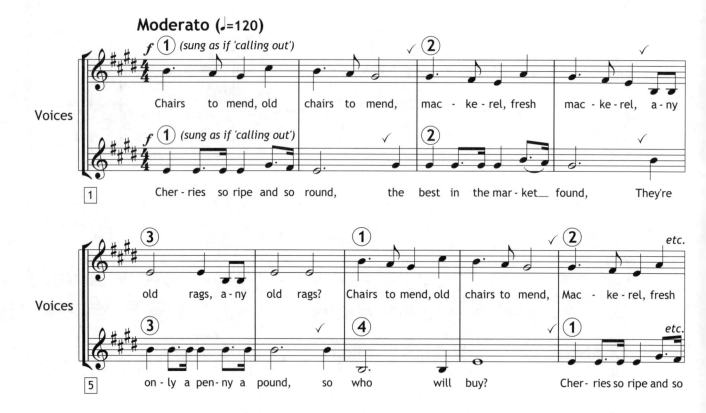

Moderato (♩=120)

(sung as if 'calling out')

Chairs to mend, old chairs to mend, mac-ke-rel, fresh mac-ke-rel, a-ny

Cher-ries so ripe and so round, the best in the mar-ket found, They're

old rags, a-ny old rags? Chairs to mend, old chairs to mend, Mac-ke-rel, fresh

on-ly a pen-ny a pound, so who will buy? Cher-ries so ripe and so

---

Notes regarding the performance of 'Street Cries'

These can be sung in a variety of ways:

i) each one in unison.
ii) each one as a round: 'Cherries So Ripe' in four parts and 'Chairs to Mend' in three parts.
iii) both sung in unison together.
iv) both sung as rounds together.

iii) & iv) would be to give the effect of an overlapping of sounds that occurs when you are at a market (as illustrated above in extract c).

Each group could have a different percussion instrument to play with them to bring out the parts.

Suggested percussion instruments: woodblocks, tambourines, drums, triangles, shakers, cymbals, xylophone etc. - whatever you have in your cupboard!

Make New Friends (a)

17th Century Round
arr. Trio Tagarela

Track 4/17

*N.B - Only the 1st descant recorder part is needed for the purposes of the play, but other parts may be included

Happy and Simple (♩=126)

Make new friends, but keep the— old,— One is sil - ver and the o - ther gold.

Make new friends, for they are— dear, Keep the old ones and the, Keep the old ones and the,

Keep the old ones and the new ones near.

Make New Friends (b)

17th Century Round
arr. Trio Tagarela

Track 5/18

Moderato (♩=120)

1. Make new friends, but keep the old,
2. Make new friends, for they are dear,

One is sil - ver and the o - ther gold.
Keep the old ones and the new ones near.

---

*Notes regarding the performance of 'Make New Friends'

Anne starts singing and Robert joins in when she reaches 3. They sing both verses as a round.

Once Anne goes back to the beginning, Cook joins in at 2., Robert at 3. (as before) and Martha & Tilly at 4. They each sing the two verses and stop once they finish the second verse, therefore they finish separately.

As each of them finishes their parts, they leave the stage: Anne first, then Cook, Robert and Martha & Tilly.

Susato's Pavane

Tylman Susato (1500-1561)

arr. Trio Tagarela

© 2003 Starshine Music

36

Strike it Up, Tabor

Thomas Weelkes (1575-1623)
arr. Trio Tagarela

Track 7/19

39

The Queen's Fanfare

Emma Murphy (2002)

Track 8

Majestically (♩=112)

D. Rec. 1

D. Rec. 2

Tr. Rec.

Ten. Rec.

Drum

Tamb.

Tuned Perc.

7

Instrumental - Galliard

Anon.
arr. Trio Tagarela

Track 9

Reprise of the piece (see p.25 of score)

Greensleeves (b)

? Henry VIII (1491-1547)
arr. Trio Tagarela

Track 10/20

Reprise of the piece **with repeats** (see p.29 of score)

© 2003 Starshine Music

41

Pastime With Good Company (a)

Henry VIII (1491-1547)
arr. Trio Tagarela

Track 11

The Queenes Alman

William Byrd (1543-1623)
arr. Trio Tagarela

* The drum part is optional - this part is not included on the backing CD

Pastime with Good Company (b)

Henry VIII (1491-1547)
arr. Trio Tagarela

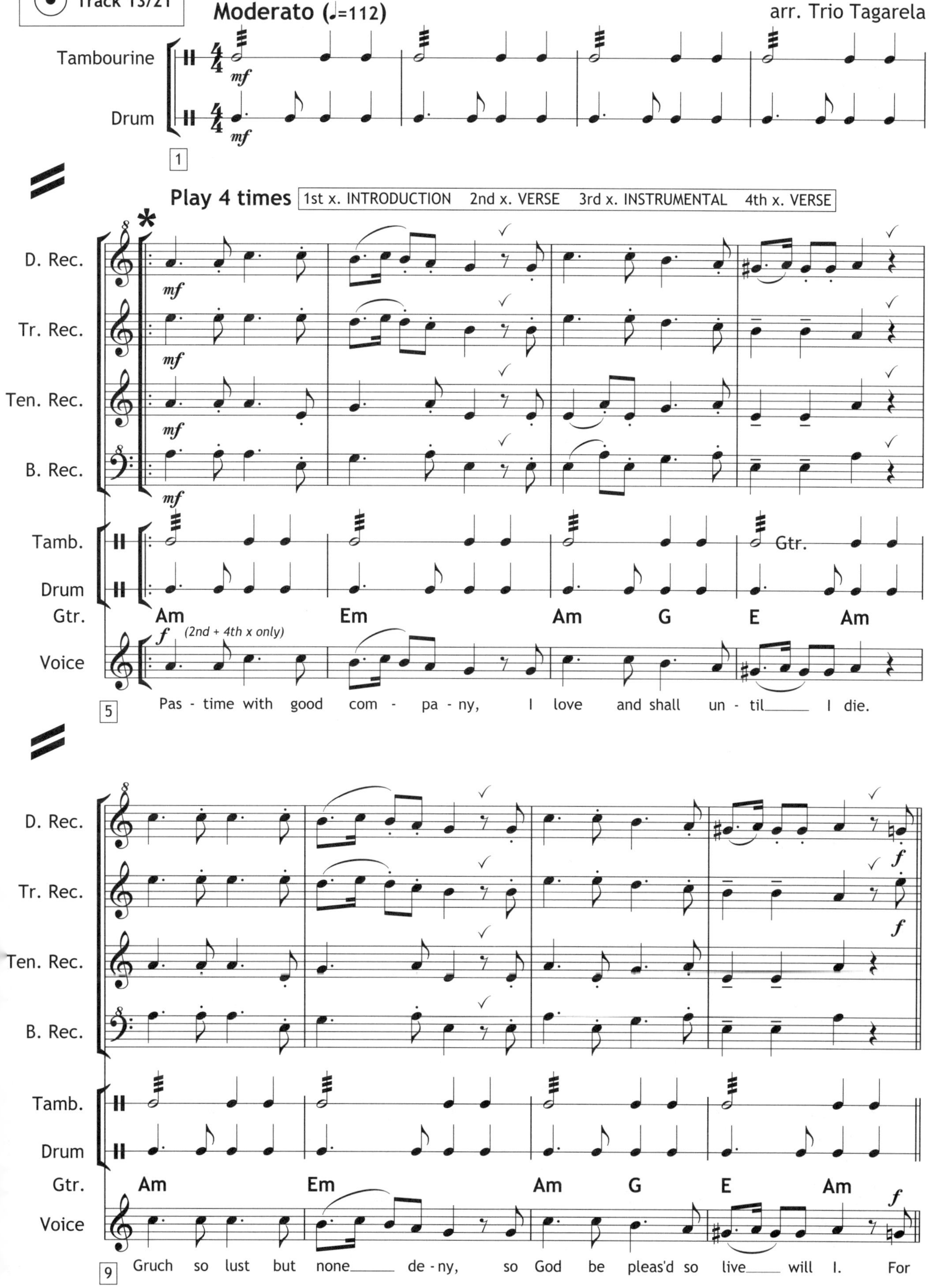

Track 13/21

Moderato (♩=112)

Play 4 times | 1st x. INTRODUCTION | 2nd x. VERSE | 3rd x. INSTRUMENTAL | 4th x. VERSE

Am   Em   Am   G   E   Am

Pas - time with good com - pa - ny, I love and shall un - til___ I die.

Am   Em   Am   G   E   Am

Gruch so lust but none___ de - ny, so God be pleas'd so live___ will I. For

45

Voice (mm. 13–16): my pas-tance, hunt, sing and dance. My heart__ is set, to my com-fort all

Voice (mm. 17–20): good-ly sport who shall__ me let?

The Pavane

The Pavane was a very popular dance during Elizabeth I's reign and would have been danced at many banquets. A common start to the dance would have been what is called a 'reverence', where dancers bow to Her Majesty, or the Lord and Lady of the house. This would happen during the musical introduction.

Reverence: The man removes his hat, and with his right foot back he bends his right knee and points his left leg forward. Meanwhile the lady bends in a curtsey, gently, as it is difficult to move much in her big dress!

Pavane steps:

1. Left, together   (a 'simple' step to the left, which is joined by the right foot.)
2. Right, together   (the same step 'mirrored')
3. Left   (steps 3-6 are called a 'Double left forward', which are steps
4. Right   starting on the left foot going forwards until the right foot joins
5. Left   the left at step 6.)
6. Together

7. Right, together   (Steps as before, mirrored)
8. Left, together
9. Right   (steps 9-12 are called a 'Double right backwards', as above mirrored.)
10. Left
11. Right
12. Together

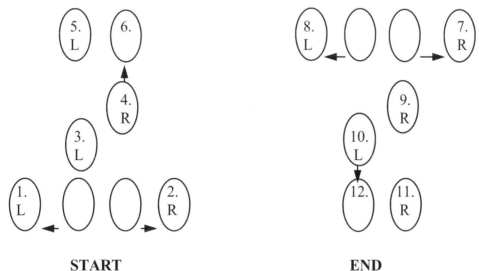

START   END

Key to Directions: R = Right Foot,   L = Left Foot,   Numbers 1-12 = steps as above
      ➤ = bring feet together

    More activities and links on the Starshine Music website: www.starshine.co.uk

Street Cries

Street cries were an early form of advertising! The louder, clearer and more interesting the cries were, the better chance a street trader had of gathering customers. Cries could be shouted or sung, and would be repeated many times in the course of a day's trading, so the crier would be very hoarse by the time they went home!

Here are some examples which you could try out, and perhaps you could make up tunes for them.

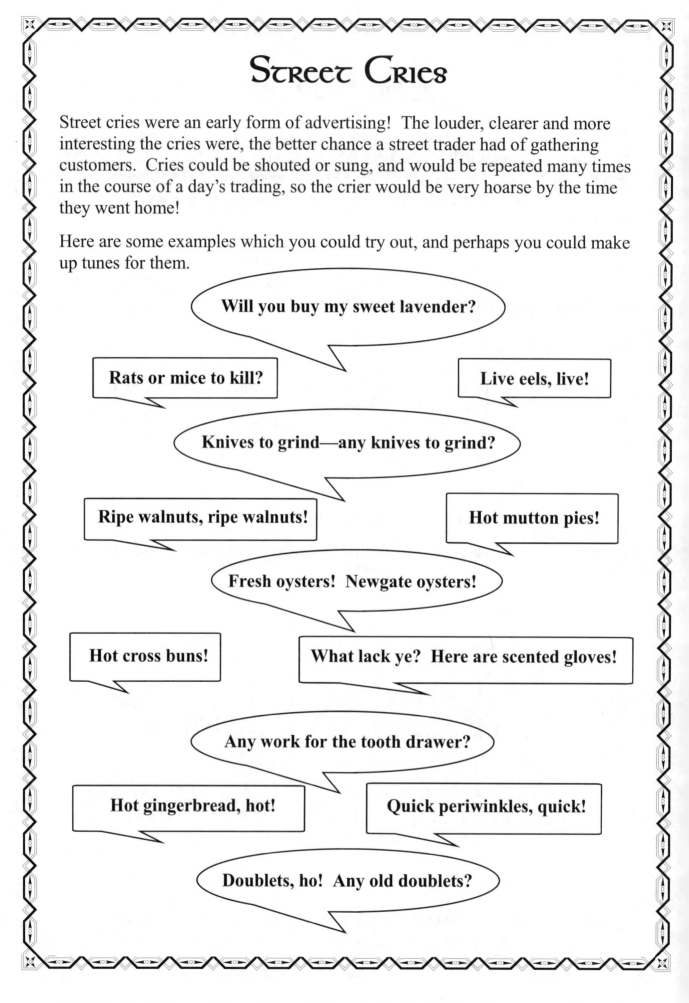

Will you buy my sweet lavender?

Rats or mice to kill?

Live eels, live!

Knives to grind—any knives to grind?

Ripe walnuts, ripe walnuts!

Hot mutton pies!

Fresh oysters! Newgate oysters!

Hot cross buns!

What lack ye? Here are scented gloves!

Any work for the tooth drawer?

Hot gingerbread, hot!

Quick periwinkles, quick!

Doublets, ho! Any old doublets?

More activities and links on the Starshine Music website: www.starshine.co.uk

Tudor Indoor Games

Table Games

In Tudor times people had to make their own entertainment, and board games or card games were popular. People played games like **Backgammon, Cards, Chess, Dice, Dominoes** and **Draughts**, which are still played today, but here are some that have gone out of fashion.

Trump

This is a game for two or more players.

1. Place a pack of cards face down on the table.
2. Turn one card over, this is called the 'trump' card.
3. Next the first player turns over one card. If that card matches the 'trump' card then all the players must hit the table with their left hand and shout "Trump!". The last person to shout and hit the table is out.
4. Each player takes a turn at turning over a card.
5. The winner is the last person left in.

Hazard

This game is played with two dice.

1. Each player has a turn at throwing the dice.
2. The person who throws the highest number is the 'caster'.
3. Next the caster throws the dice until he/she gets a 5,6,7,8 or 9. The number he gets is called the 'main point'.
4. The caster then throws again until he gets a number between 4 and 10, this is called the 'chance point'. The chance point mustn't be the same number as the main point.
5. The caster throws the dice again and tries to get the chance point, if he succeeds he is the winner, however if he/she gets the main point first then he/she loses.

This was a gambling game in Tudor times, so you could try playing for matchsticks or counters. If the caster wins, he takes one matchstick from each player. If he loses, he pays out one matchstick to each player. Once the caster loses he passes the dice to the next player who throws for a new main point and a new chance point, etc.

Tudor Indoor Games (2)

NINE MEN'S MORRIS   2 Players

Aim of the game: To capture all your opponent's pieces.

You need 9 counters, and a Nine Men's Morris Board. Players take turns to place their counters on top of the dots (points). The aim is to place **three** of your own counters in a <u>horizontal</u> or <u>vertical</u> straight line, which is called a <u>merelle</u>. If all the counters are on the board and there are no rows of three, then the players begin to move their counters around.   A counter can only be moved to an uncovered point, and by only one space. You mustn't jump over pieces, or skip points. When you get a <u>merelle</u>, you can capture one of your opponent's counters, but you aren't allowed take it from a merelle unless there are no other counters left.   You keep going until one of you has captured all the opponent's counters.

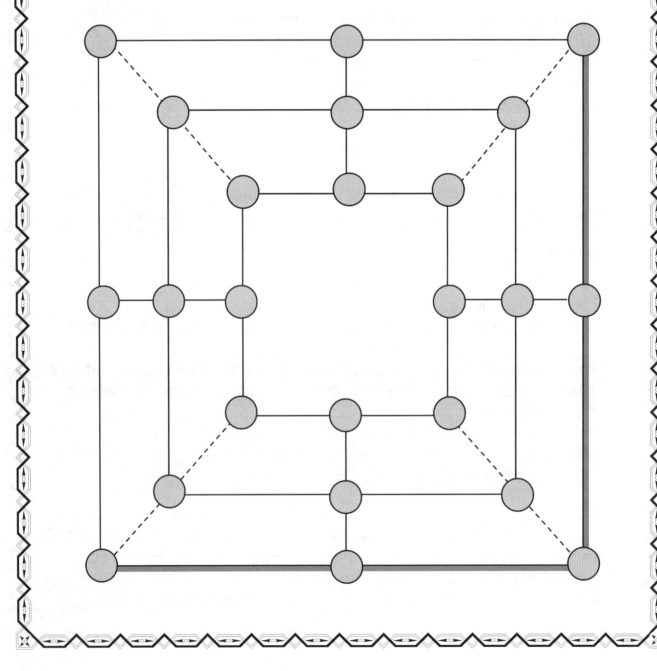

More activities and links on the Starshine Music website: <u>www.starshine.co.uk</u>

Tudor Outdoor Games

FOOTBALL

Yes, the Tudors played football! But Tudor football used to be played on a pitch several miles long. Often it was played with a starting point in between two villages, and the winning team was the one that got the ball back to their village. As there were no rules and no referee, arguments happened very often, and injuries were very common!

Either a ball of rags can be used to play with or, if you are very brave and want to be traditional, you could try using a stuffed pig's bladder!

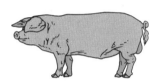

STOOLBAR

The pitch is about four metres long with two posts, one at each end. Stoolbar is played with a ball made out of rags and a stick for a bat. The aim of the game is for the bowler to stand at one post and try to throw and hit the other post with the ball. The batter must try to hit the ball, and if he does so he must then run from post to post to score runs. If, however, the bowler hits the post or a fielder catches a ball hit by the batter, the batter is out. The team that scores the most runs wins. What game is this very like?

LOGGATS

This is an easy game to learn. Push a stake into the ground then all players should stand at an agreed distance from this stick and take it in turns to throw smaller sticks, called 'loggats', at it. The winner is the person whose loggat lands closest to the stake. This game was the forerunner to some of our modern games — can you think of any?

More activities and links on the Starshine Music website: www.starshine.co.uk

Tudor Crafts (1)

How to Make Your Own Quill Pen

You will need:

1) a large strong feather
2) a sharp knife or scalpel
3) tweezers
4) a pot of ink

- Cut off some of the feathery end of your quill, shortening it to about 20cm.
- Take off all the remaining feathery bits if you wish.
- Cut the very end of the shaft off – you should ask an adult to do this for you if you are using a scalpel.
- Shape the bottom of the shaft like a pen nib (using the tweezers to take out the core).
- Make a small slit at the end of the nib about 5mm long (so that it looks like the nib of an ink pen).
- Dip the quill in ink, and write like a true Tudor!

Try copying out these Tudor Table Manners with your quill Pen:

When thou art at meat:

- Fill not thy mouth too full, lest thou must speak.
- Gulp not thy drink too fast.
- Sup not loud of thy pottage.*
- Shuffle not thy feet beneath the table, nor rest them upon it.
- Blow not on thy food to cool it.
- Thou shouldst not blow out crumbs when thou dost eat.
- Thou shalt not take all the best food for thyself.
- Spit not over the table.
- Wipe thy mouth not on the table cloth.
- Belch near no man's face with a corrupt fumosity.

Some of these words are old fashioned, but their meanings are quite easy to guess. Have a go, and check your guesses with the upside down answers below.

* There's a recipe for pea pottage on our website

thee = you	thou = youthy = you	thyself = yourself	unseemly = rude
pottage = soup	shalt = shall	shouldst = should	sup = drink (sip)
at meat = eating	corrupt fumosity = stink!	dost = do	lest = in case

More activities and links on the Starshine Music website: www.starshine.co.uk

Tudor Crafts (2)

Two Ways to Make a Ruff

Ruffs were probably the most distinctive piece of clothing of Tudor times, and certainly the most uncomfortable looking. A good ruff took a long time and great skill to make, and the bigger and fancier a person's ruff the more important and wealthy he or she appeared to be. Cleaning them wasn't easy, as you can imagine, so they probably didn't get washed very often! The real thing was made with lace, but to give the impression of a ruff you could try one of these:

1) **With paper**
    - fold about 10 pieces of paper into 'fans'
    - attach each of them together with sellotape down the ends
    - attach some white ribbon/thread/string to either side of the joined 'fans'
    - put around your neck and tie the ribbon together

2) **With white doilies**
    - take at least 8 doilies and cut them in half
    - measure your neck
    - cut a piece of ribbon twice the size of your neck
    - make the doilie halves into fans
    - attach the doilie fans to the ribbon, leaving enough ribbon at either end to tie around your neck
    - put around your neck and tie at the back

Did you know that sometimes ruffs were SO big and stuck out SO far that people found it hard to get food into their mouths?

More activities and links on the Starshine Music website: www.starshine.co.uk

Tudor Crafts (3)

How to make a Pomander

Materials needed:

1 orange with its peel still on
1 box of whole cloves
30g ground cinnamon
15g ground nutmeg
Ribbon (of any colour you wish)

Tools needed:

1 Toothpick
1 Paper bag
Scissors

Directions:

Use the toothpick to prick a hole in the skin or peel of the orange, then place a clove in the hole. Repeat this until the whole fruit is covered with cloves, preferably in one sitting because if it is left overnight it will spoil. Place it in the paper bag with the ground cinnamon and nutmeg and shake the bag until the fruit is well powdered with the spices. Put it in a warm, dry place and turn it from time to time.

The pomander should be dry in about two weeks and will have shrunk a little. Wait until it is thoroughly dry before wrapping it with ribbon and decoration. If the ribbon is made of silk or slippery, you may want to pin it to the pomander so that it stays in place.

During the Tudor Time, pomander balls were used in the kitchen, placed in baskets or cupboards to hide the bad cooking smells.

Tudor Recipes (1)

KNOTTED BISCUITS

Ingredients:
    2 eggs
    15ml caraway seeds (3 teaspoons)
    100g sugar
    175g plain flour
    Butter for greasing baking trays

Utensils:
    Mixing bowl
    Fork or whisk to beat the eggs
    Pastry board
    Saucepan
    Wire rack
    Baking trays
    Wooden spoon

Cooking:

1) Beat the eggs.
2) Add the sugar and caraway seeds and beat again.
3) Stir in the flour and mix with your hands to make a thick dough.
4) Put the dough on a floured board and knead it.
5) Roll the dough into sausage shapes 1cm wide by 10cm long.
6) Tie each strip into a knot.
7) Put a pan of water on to boil. (Do this bit with an adult.)
8) Drop some dough knots into the pan of boiling water. They will sink to the bottom, and you may need to poke them with the wooden spoon to make them float up to the top.
9) When the knots have been floating for a minute or so, take them out of the water and let them drain on a wire rack. Repeat this until all your knots have been 'floated'.
10) Put the knots on greased baking sheets and bake for 15 minutes at Gas Mark 4 (or 350 degrees F. or 180 degrees C.).
11) Turn them over and bake for another 10 minutes until they are golden brown.
12) Leave the knots to cool on the wire rack before you eat them.

Tudor Recipes (2)

Maids of honour

This recipe makes 12 'Maids of Honour Cakes'. Tradition has it that these cakes were named after Queen Elizabeth's Maids of Honour when she lived at Richmond Palace.

Ingredients for the pastry:

1 and a half cups plain flour
1 Tablespoon sugar
Half a teaspoon grated lemon peel
6 Tablespoons butter
2 Tablespoons solid lard
3 Tablespoons cold water
Pinch of salt

Ingredients for the filling:

2 Egg yolks lightly beaten
2 Tablespoons double cream
Half a cup ground almonds
Half a cup sugar
1 Tablespoon grated lemon peel
1 Tablespoon flour

Utensils: Measuring cup, 2 mixing bowls, knife, fork, greaseproof paper, 8cm pastry cutter, muffin tin

Cooking:

1) In a medium bowl, mix the flour, sugar, salt and lemon peel.
2) Put the butter and lard into the bowl, and with a knife, cut and mix it until the fat is the size of small peas.
3) Gradually sprinkle the water over the mixture, blending everything well with a fork.
4) Roll the mixture into a ball, wrap it in grease-proof paper and chill in the fridge for at least 1 hour.

5) Pre-heat the oven to 400 degrees F. or 200 degrees C.
6) In a medium bowl, mix the egg yolks, cream, almonds, sugar, lemon peel and flour.
7) Take the pastry from the fridge, and roll it on a floured board, until it is about 2mm thick
8) Cut the pastry into twelve 8cm circles.
9) Place the pastry circles into a greased muffin tin,
10) Spoon one tablespoon of filling into each prepared pastry-case.
11) Bake for 30 minutes until golden.

More activities and links on the Starshine Music website: www.starshine.co.uk

Queen Elizabeth I

Elizabeth was born on 7th September 1533, daughter of Henry VIII and his second wife, Anne Boleyn. She was third in line to the throne after her brother, Edward. He died young, and their sister, Mary, died in 1558. Elizabeth became Queen of England that year and was the last and longest-reigning Tudor monarch, dying in 1603. She was the last of the Tudors, as she never married and had no children.

"Though I have the body of a woman, I have the heart of a prince..."

Elizabeth was adored by her people, because she was a strong leader and a powerful woman. When other countries were fighting over religion, Elizabeth made sure it didn't happen in her own country. The English navy became recognised as a powerful force when the Spanish Armada was defeated in her reign.

However, the other side of Elizabeth is that she had a dreadful temper. She used to punch and kick her secretary, and she sent threatening letters to people who displeased her. She even had people executed if she thought they might be traitors.

Did you know that the Tudors were very smelly?

They must have been, because even rich people hardly ever had baths. Queen Elizabeth was very proud of the fact that she had four baths in a <u>year</u>!

Did you know that people in Tudor times had rotten teeth? Most people had them pulled out, but Queen Elizabeth was probably too scared to go to a tooth drawer because she kept her black teeth!

Tudor Clothes

Wealthy Lady   Wealthy Boy   Wealthy Girl   Wealthy Man

Poor Servant   Soldier   Market Girl

More activities and links on the Starshine Music website: www.starshine.co.uk

PERFORMING RIGHTS FOR THE SHOW

LICENCE APPLICATION

If you are planning to stage this musical, or to record the performance and/or songs, you will need to apply for a **Licence**. 'Block' licences which your school/group may have do not cover performances of musicals, licences for which are only available directly from publishers.

The revenue raised from Performing Licences is the main source of income for writers. Licence charges vary according to circumstances, but **start from** as little as £10.00 per performance, and safeguard you from prosecution. A quotation for your proposed production may be obtained from Starshine Music by phone / fax / e-mail.

To apply for a licence, complete the form below, and post or fax it to:
Starshine Music, Brown Cottage, Glynleigh Rd, Hankham, E. Sussex, England. BN24 5BJ.
Tel/Fax: +44 (0)1323 764334
Alternatively, e-mail us with the details: licences@starshine.co.uk

---

APPLICATION TO PERFORM:

TROUBLE at the TUDOR BANQUET – by Emma Murphy

Name of school / group ....

Date(s) of production ....

Venue ....

Number of performances ....

Expected audience size per performance ....

Will admissions be charged (& if so, at what rate)? ....

What form of accompaniment will you use, piano or cd/cassette? ....

Name of producer ....

Address of school / group ....

....

....

Postcode...

Daytime telephone number ....fax: ....

e-mail address ....

If you are intending to record the show, or any part of it, please estimate the number of copies you will be producing. (Include an approximate figure to cover parents making full-length video recordings, as well as any 'official' school recordings.)

VIDEO RECORDING	1-25	25-50	50-100	100+
SOUND RECORDING	1-25	25-50	50-100	100+

Index